Recipes for Success

Over 40 low point warming winter recipes

Edited by Sue Beveridge

SIMON & SCHUSTER

A VIACOM COMPANY

First published in Great Britain by
Simon & Schuster UK Ltd, 2002
A Viacom Company

Simon & Schuster UK Ltd
Africa House
64–78 Kingsway
London
WC2B 6AH

Weight Watchers Publications Manager: Corrina Griffin
Weight Watchers Publications Executive: Lucy Davidson

Editorial project manager: Anna Hitchin
Photography and styling: Tim Auty
Home economy: Becky Johnson
Designer: Jane Humphrey
Typesetting: Stylize Digital Artwork
Printed and bound in China

A CIP catalogue for this book is available from the British Library

ISBN 0 743 23134 1

Pictured on the front cover: Somerset Sausage Stew, page 21
Pictured on the back cover: Chocolate Pots with Tia Maria, page 54

All eggs, fruit and vegetables are medium-size unless otherwise
stated; teaspoons (5 ml) and tablespoons (15 ml) are level.

🅥 denotes a vegetarian recipe and assumes vegetarian cheese,
virtually fat-free fromage frais, low-fat crème fraîche and free-range
eggs are used. Virtually fat-free fromage frais and low-fat crème
fraîche may contain traces of gelatine so they are not always
vegetarian: please check the labels.

Ⓥg denotes a vegan dish.

Preparation and cooking times are approximate and meant to be
guidelines. The preparation time includes all the steps up to and
after the main cooking time(s).

contents

It's hard to believe that such delicious recipes are actually ideal for losing weight – but thanks to Weight Watchers they are! So now you can have your cake and eat it too! You'll find lots of your favourite winter dishes here – carefully re-created to be low in points and yet still taste just as good as they always have. Why not enjoy them with friends and family too? They'll never know the difference, especially when you dish up all those fabulous Christmas treats.

And speaking of Christmas – no worries! These delicious Weight Watchers recipes will see you through the season as you continue to enjoy the food you love and still lose weight. If you're entertaining, your guests will love recipes such as Smoked salmon mousse (page 12), or Chocolate pots with Tia Maria (page 54) and they'll never think it's 'diet food'. At this time of year, in the lead-up to Christmas and over the holidays, every minute is precious, so you'll be pleased to know that all the recipes are quick and easy. Many of them can also be made in advance and then frozen, if you wish.

However, this book isn't just for Christmas. There are recipes and ideas you'll want to turn to time and time again. They include satisfying main meals, warming soups and mouth-watering desserts and bakes. As you'd expect from a Weight Watchers cookbook, all the recipes give you details on preparation and cooking times, freezing information, and of course points per serving and per recipe. You'll also find a large selection of vegetarian suggestions.

So, when the supermarkets start to tempt you with high point winter treats, choose some seasonal delights from this book instead. That way you can stay in control, enjoy good food and feel wonderful in your party season outfits. With Weight Watchers **Pure Points**™ you can do it!

soups
and starters

Pumpkin soup

Farmhouse chicken and vegetable broth

Cauliflower and stilton soup

Tomato and lentil soup

Big Boston baked bean and ham soup

Smoked salmon mousse

Ham and mustard bread and butter

　puddings

Tortilla treat

Turkey cannelloni

Hot roasted vegetables

serves: **6** preparation: **15** mins cooking: **30** mins

POINTS PER SERVING

1/2

points per recipe
2 1/2

- **1 tablespoon vegetable oil**
- **1 onion, chopped**
- **600 g (1 lb 5 oz) pumpkin, peeled, de-seeded, and chopped into small chunks**
- **2 carrots, peeled and sliced**
- **1 teaspoon ground ginger**
- **1/2 teaspoon chilli powder**
- **1.2 litres (2 pints) vegetable stock**
- **1 tablespoon tomato purée**
- **1 tablespoon fresh parsley, chopped**
- **salt and freshly ground black pepper**

Pumpkin soup

1 Heat the oil in a large saucepan and gently cook the onion for 5 minutes.

2 Add the pumpkin, carrots, ginger and chilli and stir to mix. Cook for 5 more minutes.

3 Add the stock and purée to the saucepan and bring to the boil. Cover and simmer for 20 minutes or until the vegetables are soft.

4 Transfer to a liquidiser or blender and process until smooth. Alternatively, press the soup through a coarse sieve using the back of a wooden spoon.

5 Return the soup to the saucepan, reheat and check the seasoning. Serve, sprinkled with the parsley.

Freezing recommended

Farmhouse chicken and vegetable broth

1 Spray a very large saucepan with the low-fat cooking spray. Stir-fry the onion, carrots, celery and swede for 5 minutes until slightly softened. Add the pearl barley and the chicken thighs. Continue to stir-fry for 3–4 minutes or until the chicken is lightly browned.

2 Add the stock and bring to the boil, then lower the heat. Cover and simmer gently for 35–40 minutes (during this time the barley will swell and soften, absorbing some of the stock).

3 Carefully remove the cooked chicken and place on a chopping board. Add the mushrooms and sage to the saucepan and continue to simmer, covered, for about 10 minutes.

4 Meanwhile, using two forks remove the chicken from the bones and shred it into small pieces. Return the meat to the saucepan and season to taste.

5 Blend the cornflour to a paste with the Worcestershire sauce and a tablespoon of cold water. Stir into the broth and continue to heat until the broth thickens slightly. Check the seasoning.

6 Ladle the broth into warm bowls, sprinkle with the parsley and serve immediately.

Freezing recommended

points per recipe
22½

- **low-fat cooking spray**
- **1 large onion, chopped finely**
- **2 large carrots, cut into 1 cm (½-inch) slices**
- **2 sticks of celery, cut into 1 cm (½-inch) slices**
- **250 g (9 oz) swede, cut into 1 cm (½-inch) chunks**
- **65 g (2½ oz) pearl barley**
- **500 g (1 lb 2 oz) skinless chicken thighs, on the bone**
- **1.5 litres (2¾ pints) hot chicken or vegetable stock**
- **350 g (12 oz) mushrooms, sliced thickly**
- **1 teaspoon dried sage (or 1 tablespoon finely chopped fresh sage)**
- **3 tablespoons cornflour**
- **2 teaspoons Worcestershire sauce**
- **2 tablespoons chopped fresh parsley**
- **salt and freshly ground black pepper**

points per recipe
11½

- **low-fat cooking spray**
- **1 large onion, chopped**
- **2 garlic cloves, crushed**
- **½ small cauliflower, broken into florets**
- **2 vegetable stock cubes, dissolved in 850 ml (1½ pints) hot water**
- **300 ml (½ pint) skimmed milk**
- **200 g (7 oz) low-fat soft cheese**
- **2 tablespoons fresh chives, chopped**
- **50 g (1¾ oz) blue Stilton cheese, crumbled**
- **salt and freshly ground black pepper**

Cauliflower and stilton soup

1 Spray a non-stick saucepan with the low-fat cooking spray and sauté the onion and garlic for about 5 minutes, until softened.

2 Add the cauliflower and vegetable stock to the saucepan and bring up to the boil. Cover and cook over a low heat for about 20 minutes, until the cauliflower is tender.

3 Transfer the soup to a blender or food processor, add the milk then blend until smooth. Reserve 2 tablespoons of low-fat soft cheese, then add the remainder to the soup together with half the chives. Blend again to mix. Return the soup to the saucepan, add the blue cheese, then reheat gently. Season to taste.

4 Ladle the soup into warmed bowls and spoon half a tablespoon of soft cheese over the top of each serving. Sprinkle with the remaining chives, a little extra ground black pepper and then serve immediately.

Freezing recommended

Tomato and lentil soup

1 Spray a saucepan with the low-fat cooking spray, add the onion and stir-fry for 3–4 minutes.

2 Add the tomatoes, lentils, stock and cinnamon to the saucepan and stir well to mix. Cover, then simmer over a low heat for 20–25 minutes.

3 If you prefer a smooth soup, transfer the mixture to a liquidiser or blender and process for a few seconds, then return it to the saucepan and reheat gently.

4 Season to taste and serve in warmed bowls sprinkled with the fresh herbs.

Freezing recommended

- **low-fat cooking spray**
- **1 large onion, chopped**
- **400 g (14 oz) canned chopped tomatoes**
- **50 g (1¾ oz) dried split red lentils**
- **425 ml (¾ pint) vegetable stock**
- **1 teaspoon ground cinnamon**
- **1 tablespoon chopped fresh parsley or basil**
- **salt and freshly ground black pepper**

POINTS PER SERVING

2

points per recipe
3½

- **1 small onion, chopped finely**
- **205 g can of Weight Watchers from Heinz baked beans**
- **230 g (8¼ oz) canned chopped tomatoes**
- **50 g (1¾ oz) lean, cooked ham, diced finely**
- **1 teaspoon brown sugar**
- **1 teaspoon tomato purée**
- **1 teaspoon red wine vinegar**
- **dash of Tabasco or Worcestershire sauce (optional)**
- **salt and freshly ground black pepper**

Big Boston baked bean and ham soup

1 Put the onion and 3 tablespoons of water in a medium-size saucepan. Bring the water to a gentle simmer then cover and cook for a few minutes until the onion has softened.

2 Add the baked beans, tomatoes and 175 ml (6 fl oz) of cold water. Bring to the boil then add the ham, sugar, purée, vinegar and Tabasco or Worcestershire sauce, if using. Reduce the heat and leave to simmer, uncovered, for 10 minutes.

3 Season to taste then serve in warmed bowls.

Freezing not recommended

POINTS PER SERVING

2½

points per recipe
10½

- **150 g (5½ oz) smoked salmon pieces, snipped into tiny shreds**
- **finely grated zest of 1 lemon**
- **2 tablespoons fresh lemon juice**
- **1 tablespoon horseradish sauce**
- **200 g (7 oz) low-fat soft cheese**
- **1 teaspoon powdered gelatine**
- **salt and freshly ground black pepper**
- **4 thin slices of lemon or sprigs of fresh dill, to garnish**
  For the relish
- **½ cucumber, peeled and sliced in half lengthways, seeds removed**
- **1 tablespoon chopped fresh dill**
- **1 tablespoon white wine vinegar**
- **1 tablespoon caster sugar**

Smoked salmon mousse

1 Line a 500 g (1 lb 2 oz) mould (a margarine tub will do), or 4 individual ramekin dishes with clingfilm, using enough to overhang the container(s) slightly.

2 Place the salmon in a food processor with the lemon zest, juice, horseradish sauce and cheese. Blend until smooth then transfer to a mixing bowl.

3 Place 2 tablespoons of cold water in a bowl. Sprinkle the gelatine over and leave it to stand for 5 minutes, until the gelatine looks spongy. Place the bowl over a pan of gently simmering water and heat for about 2 minutes until the gelatine mixture goes clear and runny. Remove it from the heat and pour it into the salmon mixture, beating well to mix. Season to taste, then transfer the mousse to the prepared container(s) and chill in the refrigerator for at least 2 hours.

4 To prepare the relish, slice the cucumber as thinly as you can. Transfer to a bowl and toss with the chopped dill, vinegar and sugar. Chill until required.

5 To serve, arrange some of the cucumber relish on individual serving plates. Gently lift the mousse from its container(s) using the overhanging clingfilm, then discard the clingfilm. Cut the mousse into slices if necessary. Place the mousse on top of the cucumber relish and garnish with the lemon slices or sprigs of dill.

Freezing recommended for the mousse only

Ham and mustard bread and butter puddings

1 Preheat the oven to Gas Mark 5/190°C/fan oven 170°C.

2 Mix the low-fat spread and mustard together and spread over one side of each slice of bread. Cut each slice into quarters and divide between four individual ramekin dishes. Scatter the ham strips and grated cheese over the top.

3 Beat together the eggs, milk and seasoning in a mixing bowl then divide between the ramekin dishes. Put them on a baking sheet and cook for 20 minutes, until the egg mixture has set and the puddings are fluffed up and golden. Serve immediately.

Freezing not recommended

POINTS PER SERVING
2½
points per recipe
9

- **15 g (½ oz) low-fat spread, softened**
- **1 tablespoon coarse grain mustard**
- **2 slices of 2 or 3 day old, thin-cut bread, crusts removed**
- **25 g (1 oz) wafer-thin ham, cut into strips**
- **25 g (1 oz) half-fat cheddar cheese, grated**
- **2 eggs**
- **150 ml (¼ pint) skimmed milk**
- **salt and freshly ground black pepper**

serves: **6**   preparation + cooking: **35** mins

POINTS PER SERVING

2¹/₂

points per recipe
13¹/₂

- **1 teaspoon olive oil**
- **¹/₂ small onion, chopped finely**
- **1 chilli, de-seeded and chopped finely**
- **1 garlic clove, crushed**
- **400 g (14 oz) canned chopped tomatoes**
- **2 tablespoons tomato purée**
- **100 g (3¹/₂ oz) tortilla chips**
- **salt and freshly ground black pepper**
  For the topping
- **4 tomatoes, chopped**
- **1 red or green pepper, de-seeded and chopped**
- **3 spring onions, chopped**
- **1 large red chilli, de-seeded and chopped finely**
- **juice of ¹/₂ lime**
- **1 tablespoon chopped fresh coriander**
- **5 tablespoons 0% fat Greek-style yogurt**
- **75 g (2³/₄ oz) half-fat Cheddar cheese, grated**

Tortilla treat

1 Heat the oil in a large saucepan then fry the onion for a few minutes until softened. Add the chilli and garlic and cook for 1 minute more, then stir in the tomatoes and purée, and season to taste. Transfer the mixture to a food processor or blender and process until smooth. Return the mixture to the saucepan, bring to the boil then simmer for 10–15 minutes or until very thick.

2 Preheat the grill to medium.

3 Arrange the tortilla chips around the base and sides of a flameproof, shallow serving dish then spoon the tomato sauce over.

4 To make the topping, mix together the tomatoes, pepper, spring onions, chilli, lime juice and coriander. Spoon this over the sauce in the dish.

5 Place under the grill for a few minutes to heat through then spread the Greek yogurt over the top and sprinkle with the cheese. Return to the grill and heat until the cheese is melted and bubbling.

Freezing not recommended

Turkey cannelloni

1 Soak the porcini (dried mushrooms) in the boiling water for 20 minutes. Drain them, reserving the liquid, and chop them.

2 Preheat the oven to Gas Mark 6/200°C/fan oven 180°C.

3 To make the filling, spray a large frying pan with the low-fat cooking spray. Add the turkey mince, onion, garlic and seasoning and fry gently until the mince is browned all over. Add the porcini and the soaking liquid, the thyme and the Worcestershire sauce. Cook for 5 minutes or until most of the liquid has evaporated. Stir in the purée.

4 Fill the cannelloni tubes with spoonfuls of the mixture then lay them in a shallow, rectangular ovenproof dish.

5 To make the topping, mix the cornflour paste into the yogurt then add the soft cheese and season to taste. Pour this over the cannelloni and top with the grated cheese.

6 Bake in the oven for 45 minutes. Serve sprinkled with paprika.

Freezing not recommended

POINTS PER SERVING

4½

points per recipe
18

- **125 g (4½ oz) no pre-cook cannelloni tubes**
- **paprika, to serve**
  For the filling
- **15 g (½ oz) porcini**
- **75 ml (3 fl oz) boiling water**
- **low-fat cooking spray**
- **225 g (8 oz) turkey mince**
- **1 onion, diced finely**
- **2 garlic cloves, crushed**
- **1 teaspoon dried thyme**
- **½ tablespoon Worcestershire sauce**
- **1 tablespoon tomato purée**
- **salt and freshly ground black pepper**
  For the topping
- **1 teaspoon cornflour, blended with ½ tablespoon water**
- **225 ml (8 fl oz) very low-fat plain yogurt**
- **50 g (1¾ oz) low-fat soft cheese**
- **50 g (1¾ oz) half-fat Cheddar cheese, grated**

15

serves: **4**   preparation: **10** mins   cooking: **20** mins

POINTS PER SERVING

1/2

points per recipe
2

- **2 teaspoons olive oil**
- **1 courgette, sliced thinly**
- **1 yellow or red pepper, de-seeded and sliced**
- **1/2 aubergine, sliced thinly**
- **2 tomatoes, sliced**
- **1 red onion, sliced into rings**
- **2 tablespoons balsamic vinegar**
- **1 teaspoon honey**
- **1/2 teaspoon dried basil**
- **salt and freshly ground black pepper**
- **fresh basil, to garnish**

Hot roasted vegetables

1 Preheat the grill to medium. Line a baking tray or grill pan with foil and drizzle 1 teaspoon of oil over it.

2 Place all the vegetables in a single layer on the tray or grill pan.

3 Drizzle the vinegar, honey and the remaining oil over the vegetables. Sprinkle over the dried basil and season. Grill for 15–20 minutes, turning frequently, until the vegetables are softened and browned. Serve immediately, scattered with the fresh basil.

Freezing not recommended

meat,
fish and poultry

Pork with tomatoes and red wine

Turkey, ham and sweetcorn bake

Somerset sausage stew

Cranberry and orange-glazed
  gammon steaks

Beef goulash

Creamy chicken with mushrooms

Smoked mackerel hotpots

Winter seafood stew

serves: **2**   preparation: **20** mins   cooking: **20** mins

POINTS PER SERVING

2¹/₂

points per recipe
5

- **175 g (6 oz) pork tenderloin or pork fillet, cut into strips**
- **1 onion, chopped**
- **200 g (7 oz) canned chopped tomatoes with herbs**
- **75 ml (3 fl oz) red wine**
- **¹/₂ tablespoon tomato purée**
- **75 ml (3 fl oz) hot vegetable or chicken stock**
- **1 courgette, sliced thickly**
- **125 g (4¹/₂ oz) chestnut mushrooms, halved**
- **1 teaspoon dried mixed herbs**
- **1 teaspoon chopped fresh sage (or ¹/₂ teaspoon dried)**
- **1 teaspoon cornflour, blended with ¹/₂ tablespoon water**
- **salt and freshly ground black pepper**

Pork with tomatoes and red wine

1 Dry-fry the pork and onion in a large, non-stick wok or frying-pan for 5 minutes. Stir in the tomatoes, red wine, purée, stock, courgette, mushrooms and all the herbs. Bring to the boil, then cover and simmer for 20 minutes.

2 Stir the cornflour paste into the pork mixture. Simmer, uncovered, for 1–2 minutes to thicken the sauce. Season to taste and serve.

Freezing recommended

Turkey, ham and sweetcorn bake

1 Cook the potatoes in plenty of lightly salted boiling water for about 15 minutes until just tender. Drain and mash well, adding a tablespoon of the milk. Season with a little pepper.

2 Preheat the oven to Gas Mark 6/200°C/fan oven 180°C. Spray a 1 litre (1¾-pint) shallow ovenproof dish with the low-fat cooking spray.

3 Melt the margarine in a medium-size saucepan. Add the flour, stirring to blend, then cook gently for 1 minute. Remove from the heat and gradually blend in the remaining milk, then stir in the chicken stock. Return to the heat, bring to the boil, stirring continuously, and heat until the sauce thickens.

4 Add the turkey, ham, sweetcorn and parsley to the sauce. Season to taste, then pour the mixture into the prepared baking dish and top with the mashed potatoes. Bake for 25–30 minutes or until the potatoes are lightly browned. Serve garnished with the extra parsley sprinkled over the top.

Freezing recommended

POINTS PER SERVING
6½
points per recipe
12½

- **350 g (12 oz) potatoes, peeled and cut into chunks**
- **150 ml (¼ pint) skimmed milk**
- **low-fat cooking spray**
- **25 g (1 oz) polyunsaturated margarine**
- **25 g (1 oz) plain flour**
- **150 ml (¼ pint) chicken stock**
- **175 g (6 oz) cooked turkey, cut into chunks**
- **25 g (1 oz) cooked ham, chopped**
- **50 g (1¾ oz) canned or frozen sweetcorn**
- **½ tablespoon chopped fresh parsley, plus extra sprigs to garnish**
- **salt and freshly ground black pepper**

Somerset sausage stew

1 Brown the sausages by dry-frying them in a large saucepan for 2–3 minutes, turning frequently. Add the leeks, celery, carrots and pepper. Cover and cook for a further 2–3 minutes, shaking the pan occasionally to prevent the contents sticking to the bottom.

2 Stir in the tomatoes, purée and cider. Bring to the boil, then cover and simmer for 15 minutes.

3 Stir the cornflour paste into the casserole, then add the mushrooms and sage. Simmer, uncovered, for a further 10 minutes or until the vegetables are tender. Season to taste then serve with mashed potatoes.

Freezing recommended

POINTS PER SERVING

6

points per recipe
23

- **450 g (1 lb) reduced-fat sausages**
- **2 leeks, sliced**
- **2 celery sticks, sliced**
- **2 carrots, sliced thinly**
- **1 green pepper, de-seeded and sliced**
- **2 × 400 g (14 oz) cans of chopped tomatoes with herbs**
- **1 tablespoon tomato purée**
- **150 ml (¼ pint) dry cider**
- **1 tablespoon cornflour, blended with 3 tablespoons water**
- **175 g (6 oz) chestnut mushrooms, sliced**
- **1 tablespoon chopped fresh sage (or 1 teaspoon dried)**
- **salt and freshly ground black pepper**
- **400 g (14 oz) mashed potatoes, to serve**

serves: **2**   preparation + cooking: **20** mins

POINTS PER SERVING

6

points per recipe
12

- **2 × 150 g (5½ oz) lean gammon steaks**
- **2 tablespoons cranberry sauce**
- **2 cloves, stalks removed then crushed**
- **4 thin slices of orange, to garnish**

Cranberry and orange-glazed gammon steaks

1 Preheat the grill to medium. Grill the gammon steaks for 5 minutes on each side, or until cooked through.

2 Meanwhile, put the cranberry sauce in a small bowl and blend in the crushed cloves. Either heat in the microwave on High for 10 seconds, or transfer to a small saucepan and heat on the hob until hot.

3 Remove the steaks from the grill and increase the heat to high. Spread each steak with a tablespoon of the warmed cranberry and clove mixture and top each with two slices of orange. Flash the steaks under the grill briefly then serve immediately.

Freezing recommended

Beef goulash

1 Heat the oil in a medium-size saucepan and fry the onion until softened. Add the steak and cook, stirring occasionally, until it is sealed on all sides.

2 Stir in the paprika, bay leaves, wine, tomatoes and stock and bring to the boil. Season to taste. Simmer, covered, for 30 minutes then uncovered for a further 30 minutes or until the meat is tender and the sauce has thickened.

3 Sprinkle with the parsley just before serving.

Freezing recommended

POINTS PER SERVING

3

points per recipe
11½

- **1 teaspoon olive oil**
- **1 onion, sliced**
- **350 g (12 oz) lean stewing steak, cubed**
- **1 tablespoon paprika**
- **2 bay leaves**
- **150 ml (¼ pint) red wine**
- **400 g (14 oz) canned chopped tomatoes**
- **150 ml (¼ pint) beef stock**
- **1 tablespoon chopped fresh parsley**
- **salt and freshly ground black pepper**

serves: **4**   preparation + cooking: **30** mins

POINTS PER SERVING
2½
points per recipe
10

- **2 teaspoons olive oil**
- **6 shallots, quartered**
- **1 green pepper, de-seeded and diced**
- **2 × 165 g (5¾ oz) skinless, boneless chicken breasts, cut into strips**
- **2 heaped teaspoons whole-grain mustard**
- **250 g (9 oz) mushrooms, sliced**
- **295 g can 99% fat-free Campbell's Condensed Chicken Soup**
- **150 ml (¼ pint) skimmed milk**
- **salt and freshly ground black pepper**

Creamy chicken with mushrooms

1 Heat the oil in a wok or non-stick saucepan then add the shallots and pepper and fry for about 1 minute.

2 Add the chicken and the mustard and stir-fry for about 5 minutes, until the chicken turns brown.

3 Add the mushrooms and stir-fry for a few minutes more, adding a little hot water if the mixture begins to stick.

4 Add the soup and skimmed milk. Heat through, adding some hot water if you prefer a thinner sauce. Season to taste then serve.

Freezing recommended

Smoked mackerel hotpots

1 Heat the oil in a saucepan then fry the onion, celery and courgette for 5 minutes.

2 Meanwhile, warm four 10 cm (4-inch) ramekin dishes or one 850 ml (1½-pint) shallow, flameproof dish. Preheat the grill to medium. In a small bowl mix together the breadcrumbs and grated cheese.

3 Remove the onion mixture from the heat then stir in the flaked mackerel and tomatoes. Blend the lemon juice and soft cheese together and fold this into the mackerel mixture. Season to taste.

4 Spoon the mackerel mixture into the warmed dish(es), and evenly spread the cheesy breadcrumbs over the surface.

5 Grill for 4–5 minutes or until the breadcrumbs are golden and the cheese is bubbling. Serve immediately.

Freezing not recommended

POINTS PER SERVING
7½
points per recipe
29½

- **1 teaspoon vegetable oil**
- **1 small onion, chopped finely**
- **2 celery sticks, chopped finely**
- **1 courgette, diced finely**
- **25 g (1 oz) fresh breadcrumbs**
- **25 g (1 oz) half-fat Cheddar cheese, grated**
- **350 g (12 oz) smoked mackerel fillets, skinned and flaked**
- **4 tomatoes, de-seeded and chopped finely**
- **juice of ¼ lemon**
- **4 tablespoons low-fat soft cheese**
- **salt and freshly ground black pepper**

POINTS PER SERVING

3½

points per recipe
14½

- **1 tablespoon olive oil**
- **2 shallots or 1 onion, chopped finely**
- **425 ml (¾ pint) good quality fish or vegetable stock**
- **4 tablespoons white wine**
- **large pinch of saffron strands (optional)**
- **grated zest of ½ lemon**
- **225 g (8 oz) salmon fillets, skinned and cut into 4 cm (1½-inch) chunks**
- **225 g (8 oz) haddock fillets, skinned and cut into 4 cm (1½-inch) chunks**
- **2 tablespoons half-fat crème fraîche**
- **100 g (3½ oz) cooked, peeled prawns**
- **salt and freshly ground black pepper**
- **1 tablespoon chopped fresh parsley or dill, to garnish**

Winter seafood stew

1 Heat the oil in a large saucepan and gently fry the shallots or onion for 4–5 minutes, until softened but not coloured.

2 Add the stock, wine, saffron, if using, and lemon zest and season lightly. Heat until simmering gently, then add the salmon and haddock. Cover the saucepan and poach for 2–3 minutes or until the fish becomes opaque. Carefully remove the fish from the saucepan and set it aside, keeping it warm.

3 Boil the stock rapidly to reduce it to approximately 200 ml (7 fl oz). Stir in the crème fraîche and prawns then return the fish to the saucepan. Heat through for 3–4 minutes, and adjust the seasoning to taste. Serve garnished with the parsley or dill.

Freezing not recommended

vegetarian
dishes

Red lentil and sweet pepper curry

Mexican bean wraps

Mushroom risotto bake

Roasted vegetable tagliatelle

Festive vegetable bourguignon

Shepherdess pie

Macaroni cheese and mushroom crumble

Potato and onion cake

Colourful couscous casserole

serves: **4**   preparation: **30** mins   cooking: **45** mins

3½

POINTS PER SERVING

points per recipe
13½

- **2 teaspoons sunflower oil**
- **1 onion, chopped**
- **2 garlic cloves, crushed**
- **2 tablespoons curry powder**
- **150 g (5½ oz) dried red lentils**
- **1 red pepper, de-seeded and chopped**
- **1 green pepper, de-seeded and chopped**
- **1 yellow pepper, de-seeded and chopped**
- **1 aubergine, diced**
- **600 ml (1 pint) vegetable stock**
- **200 g (7 oz) canned chopped tomatoes**
- **2 tablespoons chopped fresh coriander**
- **50 g (1¾ oz) almond flakes, toasted**
- **salt and freshly ground black pepper**

Red lentil and sweet pepper curry

1 Heat the oil in a large saucepan and cook the onion and garlic until softened. Stir in the curry powder and cook for a further minute.

2 Stir in the lentils, peppers and aubergine, then pour the stock over and bring to the boil. Cover, reduce the heat and simmer for 30 minutes, until the lentils are tender, stirring from time to time.

3 Remove the lid from the pan, stir in the tomatoes, season and allow to bubble for 15 minutes or until the desired thickness is achieved. Stir in the coriander, scatter with the almonds then serve.

Freezing recommended

POINTS PER SERVING
6½
points per recipe
12½

- **low-fat cooking spray**
- **1 small onion, sliced finely**
- **1 garlic clove, crushed**
- **220 g can of chick-peas, drained**
- **215 g can of kidney beans in chilli sauce**
- **200 g (7 oz) canned chopped tomatoes**
- **4 × small (15 cm/6-inch) soft flour tortillas**
- **salt and freshly ground black pepper**

Mexican bean wraps

1 Spray a non-stick saucepan with the low-fat cooking spray then gently fry the onion and garlic until soft, but not browned.

2 Add the chick-peas, kidney beans with their sauce and the tomatoes. Mix well and heat through then season to taste.

3 Meanwhile, warm the tortillas in the microwave or under a preheated grill for a few seconds, according to the packet instructions.

4 Place a serving of the bean mixture in the middle of each tortilla, then gently roll the tortilla up and serve warm.

Freezing recommended (freeze the bean mixture and tortillas in separate containers)

Mushroom risotto bake

1 Heat the oil in a large, heavy-based saucepan and fry the onion for 2 minutes. Add the garlic and mushrooms and gently fry for a further 10 minutes, stirring frequently.

2 Stir in the rice. Add a ladleful of stock and cook until the liquid has been absorbed. Repeat this process until the rice is tender and all the stock has been absorbed — this will take 30–40 minutes. Remove the saucepan from the heat.

3 Towards the end of the cooking time, preheat the grill and warm a flameproof dish under it.

4 Add the parsley and half the cheese to the rice mixture and season to taste. Spoon into the warmed dish. Mix the remaining cheese with the breadcrumbs and sprinkle this over the top.

5 Grill for a few minutes, until the topping is golden, then serve.

Freezing not recommended

POINTS PER SERVING
4
points per recipe
16

- **1 teaspoon olive oil**
- **1 onion, chopped finely**
- **2 garlic cloves, crushed**
- **175 g (6 oz) large open cap mushrooms, chopped**
- **175 g (6 oz) button mushrooms, sliced**
- **175 g (6 oz) chestnut mushrooms, sliced**
- **125 g (4¹/2 oz) shiitake mushrooms, sliced**
- **225 g (8 oz) risotto rice**
- **700 ml (1¹/4 pints) vegetable stock**
- **2 tablespoons chopped fresh parsley**
- **50 g (1³/4 oz) half-fat Cheddar cheese, grated finely**
- **15 g (¹/2 oz) fresh white breadcrumbs**
- **salt and freshly ground black pepper**

serves: **2**   preparation + cooking: **55** mins

POINTS PER SERVING

6

points per recipe
12

- **1 tablespoon olive oil**
- **3 parsnips, diced**
- **1 fennel bulb, diced**
- **4 celery sticks, diced**
- **1 onion, chopped**
- **3 large carrots, diced**
- **600 ml (1 pint) hot vegetable stock**
- **150 ml (¼ pint) white wine**
- **100 g (3½ oz) quick-cook tagliatelle, broken into pieces**
- **2 tablespoons fresh basil, torn into small pieces**
- **salt and freshly ground black pepper**
- **2 tablespoons ready-made tomato salsa, to serve**

Roasted vegetable tagliatelle

1 Preheat the oven to Gas Mark 6/200°C/fan oven 180°C.

2 Heat the oil on the hob in a large ovenproof saucepan or casserole dish. Add the parsnips, fennel, celery, onion and carrots and fry for 2 minutes.

3 Transfer the saucepan or dish to the oven and bake, uncovered, for 20–25 minutes.

4 Remove the saucepan or dish from the oven and return to the hob. Pour in the stock and wine, season to taste and bring to the boil. Simmer for 2 minutes, then stir in the tagliatelle and basil.

5 Cover the pan and cook for a further 4–5 minutes, or until the pasta is cooked. Serve in individual bowls topped with a tablespoon of salsa.

Freezing not recommended

Festive vegetable bourguignon

1 Preheat the oven to Gas Mark 3/160°C/fan oven 140°C.

2 Place all the vegetables, prunes and chestnuts in a large bowl. Sprinkle them with the flour and add salt to taste. Toss them until they are evenly coated.

3 On the hob, heat a teaspoon of the oil in a large ovenproof saucepan or casserole dish. Add the garlic and a third of the vegetable mixture and heat until browned. Remove from the saucepan or dish and set aside, then repeat twice more until all the remaining oil and vegetable mixture has been used. Return all the vegetable mixture to the saucepan and pour the stock and wine over. Tuck in the bouquet garni and add salt to taste.

4 Bring to the boil on the hob, cover, then transfer to the oven and bake for 35 minutes or until the vegetables are tender.

5 Remove from the oven, divide the vegetables between four shallow bowls, discarding the bouquet garni, and set to one side but keep them warm. Return the saucepan or dish to the hob and rapidly boil the remaining juices, uncovered, until reduced to a syrupy consistency. Check to see if you need to add more salt then spoon the juices over the warm vegetables. Serve immediately.

Freezing not recommended

POINTS PER SERVING

4

points per recipe
16

- **225 g (8 oz) sweet potato, peeled and cut into 5 cm (2-inch) chunks**
- **225 g (8 oz) small parsnips, peeled and cut in half lengthways**
- **225 g (8 oz) button mushrooms, left whole**
- **225 g (8 oz) baby carrots, trimmed**
- **8 shallots, peeled**
- **175 g pack of baby leeks, trimmed**
- **125 g (4½ oz) ready-to-eat prunes**
- **125 g (4½ oz) vacuum-packed cooked, peeled chestnuts**
- **25 g (1 oz) plain flour**
- **3 teaspoons olive oil**
- **2 garlic cloves, crushed**
- **400 ml (14 fl oz) hot vegetable stock**
- **200 ml (7 fl oz) red wine**
- **1 bouquet garni**
- **salt**

Shepherdess pie

1 Preheat the oven to Gas Mark 6/200°C/fan oven 180°C.

2 Heat the oil in a large saucepan and gently heat the leek, courgette, carrot, garlic and mushrooms. Once warmed through, cover and cook, stirring frequently, for 10 minutes, or until the vegetables are soft.

3 Add the lentils, tomatoes, herbs and 425 ml (¾ pint) water. Bring the mixture to the boil, then reduce the heat and simmer, partially covered, for 30 minutes or until the lentils are soft and the mixture is thick. Stir in the brown sauce and baked beans and cook for a further 5 minutes.

4 Meanwhile, boil the potatoes in a saucepan of salted water for about 20 minutes, or until tender. Drain thoroughly, add the milk and mash until smooth.

5 Spoon the lentil mixture into a large, ovenproof dish. Spread the mashed potatoes over the top and sprinkle with the grated cheese.

6 Bake in the oven for 15–20 minutes or until the potato is crispy. Serve immediately.

Freezing recommended

POINTS PER SERVING

5½

points per recipe
22½

- **2 teaspoons sunflower oil**
- **1 leek, chopped finely**
- **1 small courgette, diced**
- **1 carrot, diced**
- **1 garlic clove, crushed**
- **125 g (4½ oz) mushrooms, sliced**
- **60 g (2 oz) dried split red lentils**
- **60 g (2 oz) dried green lentils**
- **200 g (7 oz) canned chopped tomatoes**
- **½ teaspoon dried marjoram**
- **½ teaspoon dried thyme**
- **1½ tablespoons brown sauce**
- **200 g can of reduced-sugar baked beans**
- **1 kg (2 lb 4 oz) potatoes, peeled and cut into chunks**
- **5–6 tablespoons skimmed milk**
- **25 g (1 oz) half-fat Cheddar cheese, grated**

serves: **4**   preparation: **20** mins   cooking: **20** mins

points per recipe
16

- **225 g (8 oz) quick-cook macaroni**
- **175 g (6 oz) button mushrooms, halved**
- **295 g can of Weight Watchers from Heinz Tomato Soup**
- **4 tomatoes, sliced**
- **25 g (1 oz) fresh wholemeal breadcrumbs**
- **50 g (1¾ oz) half-fat Cheddar cheese, grated**
- **salt and freshly ground black pepper**

Macaroni cheese and mushroom crumble

1 Preheat the oven to Gas Mark 6/200°C/fan oven 180°C.

2 Cook the macaroni in a large saucepan of lightly salted boiling water for 5 minutes, or according to the packet instructions. Drain well then return it to the saucepan.

3 Add the mushrooms and tomato soup to the saucepan and warm the mixture through, stirring well. Season to taste.

4 Transfer the macaroni mixture to an ovenproof dish, top with the sliced tomatoes and some extra seasoning.

5 Mix the breadcrumbs with the cheese then sprinkle them over the top before baking for 20 minutes.

Freezing recommended (without the tomato and crumble topping)

Potato and onion cake

V

1 Preheat the oven to Gas Mark 6/200°C/fan oven 180°C. Line a 1.5 litre (2³/4-pint) round, ovenproof dish with foil or baking parchment and spray with the low-fat cooking spray.

2 In a small saucepan mix the mushrooms, onion and garlic together. Add a teaspoon of the oil and a tablespoon of the milk and heat for 5 minutes. Season to taste.

3 Slice the potatoes thinly, but do not rinse them.

4 Place a third of the potatoes over the bottom of the dish. Season well. Layer half the mushroom mixture over the potatoes, then add another third of potatoes. Season again. Spread the remaining half of the mushroom mixture on top, then, finally, the remaining potatoes.

5 Pour the remaining milk over. Brush the top with the remaining oil. Cover with foil. Bake for 45 minutes, removing the foil for the last 15 minutes. The top should be brown and crispy, the potatoes soft.

6 Remove the dish from the oven and allow to rest for 5 minutes. Preheat the grill.

7 Invert the potato and onion cake onto a ovenproof plate and remove the foil or parchment. Put it under a grill for a few minutes to crisp and brown the base a little, then serve immediately.

Freezing recommended

POINTS PER SERVING

3¹/2

points per recipe
7

- **low-fat cooking spray**
- **100 g (3¹/2 oz) mixed mushrooms, sliced (e.g. button, oyster, field, shiitake)**
- **1 onion, chopped**
- **1 garlic clove, crushed**
- **1 tablespoon vegetable oil**
- **75 ml (3 fl oz) skimmed milk**
- **350 g (12 oz) potatoes, peeled**
- **salt and freshly ground black pepper**

serves: **2**   preparation: **30** mins   cooking: **45** mins

3½

points per serving

points per recipe
6½

- **125 g (4½ oz) couscous**
- **75 ml (3 fl oz) boiling water**
- **1 large onion, chopped**
- **75 ml (3 fl oz) hot vegetable stock**
- **2 garlic cloves, crushed**
- **1 leek, sliced very finely**
- **2 different coloured peppers, de-seeded and chopped**
- **50 g (1¾ oz) broccoli, broken into tiny florets**
- **4 mushrooms, sliced**
- **75 g (2¾ oz) baby corn**
- **400 g (14 oz) canned chopped tomatoes**
- **4 tomatoes, sliced**
- **salt and freshly ground black pepper**

Colourful couscous casserole

1 Put the couscous in a mixing bowl and add the boiling water, stirring to mix. Cover and put to one side for 5 minutes. Meanwhile, bring the onion, stock and garlic to the boil in a large saucepan then simmer for 5 minutes.

2 Preheat the oven to Gas Mark 4/180°C/fan oven 160°C and warm a large casserole dish.

3 Stir the couscous into the onion mixture in the saucepan, then stir in the remaining ingredients, except the fresh tomatoes. Season to taste then heat until nearly boiling.

4 Transfer the mixture to the warm casserole dish and arrange the sliced tomatoes on the top. Cover with a lid or foil and bake for 45 minutes. Serve immediately.

Freezing not recommended

Christmas
favourites

Baby coronation potato bites

Ham and mushroom Christmas
    crackers

Roast turkey with Madeira sauce

Herb and lemon stuffing

De-luxe mince parcels

Merry Christmas pudding

Christmas pudding ice cream

Cranberry muffins

Christmas cake

POINTS PER POTATO BITE
1/2
points per recipe
7 1/2

- **8 small potatoes (total weight approx 250 g/9 oz)**
- **1 tablespoon olive oil**
- **coarsely ground rock salt**
- **freshly ground black pepper**
  For the topping
- **50 g (1 3/4 oz) cooked chicken, diced**
- **2 tablespoons chopped red pepper**
- **4 tablespoons very low-fat plain fromage frais**
- **2 teaspoons curry paste**
- **2 teaspoons mango chutney**
- **fresh parsley, to garnish**

Baby coronation potato bites

1 Preheat the oven to Gas Mark 5/190°C/fan oven 170°C and heat a shallow roasting tin for 5 minutes.

2 Put the potatoes in a plastic bag with the oil. Grind the salt and pepper generously into the bag and shake until they are well covered. Tip them into the preheated tin and roast for 30–40 minutes, shaking the tin occasionally, until cooked.

3 Meanwhile, make the topping by simply combining all the ingredients together, except the parsley.

4 When the potatoes are cooked, put them to one side until just before you want to serve them – you can prepare them up to 2 hours in advance since they can be served slightly warm or at room temperature. To serve, cut them in half and top each of them with a spoonful of the chicken mixture. Garnish with the parsley and serve immediately.

Freezing not recommended

Ham and mushroom Christmas crackers

1 Preheat the oven to Gas Mark 6/200°C/fan oven 180°C. Spray two baking sheets with the low-fat cooking spray.

2 Put the soft cheese in a mixing bowl and beat until smooth. Add half the beaten egg and mix well, then stir in the ham, mushrooms and spring onions. Season to taste.

3 Lay the sheets of filo pastry on a clean, dry surface and cut each in half to make two squares. Cover three of the squares to prevent them from drying out, and brush around the edges of the other square with some olive oil. Spoon a quarter of the cheese mixture on to the prepared pastry square, in a sausage shape, about 2 cm (3/4-inch) in from the edge nearest you. Leave about 5 cm (2 inches) at the sides to form the 'cracker' ends.

4 Starting with the edge nearest to you, roll the pastry and filling into a tube shape. Do this fairly loosely or the cracker could split when cooking. Twist or gather the ends to form a 'cracker' shape. Place on a baking tray then repeat with the other squares of pastry.

5 Gently brush the 'crackers' with the remaining egg. Bake for about 20 minutes or until puffed and golden brown. Ideal as a starter.

Freezing recommended

POINTS PER SERVING

3

points per recipe
11½

- low-fat cooking spray
- **200 g (7 oz) low-fat soft cheese**
- **1 egg, beaten**
- **75 g (2¾ oz) ham, chopped**
- **50 g (1¾ oz) mushrooms (preferably mixed exotic mushrooms such as shiitake, oyster, portabello or brown mushrooms), sliced thinly**
- **½ tablespoon chopped spring onions**
- **2 sheets of filo pastry (50 × 24 cm/20 × 9½ inches), thawed and kept covered until required**
- **1 teaspoon olive oil**
- **salt and freshly ground black pepper**

serves: **4**   preparation: **20** mins   cooking: **1¼-1½** hrs

POINTS PER SERVING

4

points per recipe
15½

- **800 g (1 lb 11 oz) boneless turkey breast joint, skin removed**
- **2 teaspoons dried mixed herbs**
- **1 onion, quartered and stuck with cloves**
- **2 tablespoons plain flour**
- **300 ml (½ pint) chicken stock**
- **4 tablespoons Madeira or Marsala wine or sweet sherry**
- **salt and freshly ground black pepper**

Roast turkey with Madeira sauce

1 Preheat the oven to Gas Mark 4/180°C/fan oven 160°C, or according to the cooking instructions given with the meat.

2 Rub the turkey with the herbs and some salt and pepper.

3 Place the onion in a roasting tin and position the joint on top of it. Cover with foil and roast for 1¼–1½ hours. Test if it is ready by inserting a skewer into the thickest part of the meat – the juices should run clear. If not, put the joint back in the oven for a little longer then test again.

4 Transfer the joint to a carving tray, reserving the pan juices, cover with foil and leave to stand while you make the gravy.

5 Sift the flour into the pan juices and add the stock and wine or sherry. Boil briskly on the hob for 5 minutes. Season to taste.

6 Carve the turkey and serve the sauce separately, or pour it over the sliced meat.

Freezing recommended

Herb and lemon stuffing

1 Preheat the oven to Gas Mark 4/180°C/fan oven 160°C.

2 Place the onion in a small pan with a little lightly salted boiling water. Cover and boil for 5 minutes then drain.

3 Combine the onion, breadcrumbs, lemon zest and herbs in a mixing bowl then season well. Add the egg and mix thoroughly. Divide the mixture into six and roll into small balls. Place on a baking tray or in a small, shallow cake tin.

4 Cook in the oven for 30–40 minutes until firm and brown.

Freezing recommended for up to 2 months

POINTS PER SERVING

1

points per recipe
5

- **1 small onion, chopped very finely**
- **100 g (3½ oz) fresh white breadcrumbs**
- **finely grated zest of 1 lemon**
- **3 tablespoons chopped fresh herbs (e.g. parsley, thyme, sage, rosemary)**
- **1 egg, beaten**
- **salt and freshly ground black pepper**

De-luxe mince parcels

1 Preheat the oven to Gas Mark 6/200°C/fan oven 180°C.

2 In a mixing bowl combine the mincemeat and fruit together then set aside.

3 Lay a sheet of filo pastry on a clean, dry work surface. Cut it into 2 squares, then cut each of these squares into 3 rectangular strips.

4 Place 3 strips randomly on top of each other so that the corners point in different directions. Brush the edges with egg then place a spoonful of the mincemeat mixture in the centre. Scrunch the edges together to form a ruffle and place the parcel into a section of a non-stick bun tin, or on a non-stick baking tray.

5 Repeat the process with the remaining pastry and mincemeat, then gently brush the parcels with the remaining egg. Bake them for 6–10 minutes, until golden brown. Serve warm, lightly dusted with icing sugar.

Freezing not recommended

POINTS PER PARCEL
1½
points per recipe
15½

- **125 g (4½ oz) mincemeat**
- **2 small ripe bananas, diced finely**
- **1 dessert apple, peeled, cored and grated**
- **6 sheets filo pastry (50 × 24 cm/20 × 9½ inches), thawed and kept covered until required**
- **1 egg, beaten**
- **2 teaspoons icing sugar, to dust**

points per recipe
22

- **150 g (5¹/₂ oz) seedless raisins**
- **100 g (3¹/₂ oz) currants**
- **boiling water, to cover raisins and currants**
- **100 ml (3¹/₂ fl oz) brandy or rum**
- **100 g (3¹/₂ oz) parsnip, grated finely**
- **75 g (2³/₄ oz) fresh wholemeal breadcrumbs**
- **finely grated zest and juice of 1 orange**
- **1 teaspoon ground mixed spice**
- **50 g (1³/₄ oz) molasses sugar**
- **1 egg, beaten**
- **¹/₂ teaspoon polyunsaturated margarine**

Merry Christmas pudding

1 Put the raisins and currants in a large mixing bowl. Just cover with boiling water then leave to soak for 5 minutes. Drain well then add the brandy or rum, cover, and leave to soak for 6−8 hours or overnight.

2 Add all the remaining ingredients to the mixing bowl, except the margarine, and mix thoroughly. Use the margarine to grease an 850 ml (1¹/₂ pint) pudding basin then spoon in the pudding mixture. Level the surface, then cover the mixture with a circle of greaseproof paper which fits inside the basin. Cover the top of the basin with foil or greaseproof paper and secure it firmly with string.

3 Put the basin in a steamer pan over simmering water and steam for 5 hours. Top up with extra boiling water as required to prevent the pudding from boiling dry. (Alternatively, the pudding could be steamed in a slow cooker. Preheat it according to the manufacturer's instructions, place the basin inside and pour in boiling water to reach half way up the basin. Cook on high for 12 hours.)

4 Remove the basin from the saucepan (or slow cooker). Allow to cool then replace the foil or greaseproof paper with new pieces. Store in a cool, dark place − the pudding will keep for 2 months.

5 To re-heat before serving, steam for 2 hours (see step 3).

Freezing not recommended

Christmas pudding ice cream

V if using vegetarian Christmas pudding

1 Put the sugar and rum or brandy in a small saucepan and heat gently until the sugar has dissolved. Put the dried fruit in a large mixing bowl, pour the sugar and rum mixture over then leave to soak for a few hours (or overnight) until the fruit is plump.

2 Meanwhile, warm the pudding through in the microwave on High for 30–60 seconds or on a baking tray in an oven, preheated to Gas Mark 4/180°C/fan oven 160°C for 15 minutes. Chop it into small pieces then leave until cooled (about 20 minutes).

3 When the fruit is ready, mix the chilled low-fat custard with the fromage frais in a large, clean bowl. Add the chopped pudding and then the fruit, with its soaking liquid. Stir well.

4 Transfer to an ice cream machine and churn for 30–40 minutes (or according to the machine instructions). Then transfer to a freezer container and put in the freezer for a couple of hours to finish the freezing process. If you do not have an ice cream machine, beat well and then transfer to a freezer container. Leave until nearly frozen (2–3 hours), then remove from the freezer, beat well again and allow to finish freezing for another 2–3 hours.

5 Remove from the freezer 15 minutes before serving.

Freezing required

POINTS PER SERVING
3½
points per recipe
20

- **1 tablespoon dark muscovado sugar**
- **50 ml (2 fl oz) rum or brandy**
- **50 g (1¾ oz) dried fruit of your choice (e.g. mixed dried fruit or raisins)**
- **100 g (3½ oz) left-over Christmas Pudding**
- **300 ml (½ pint) ready-made, low-fat custard, chilled**
- **350 g (12 oz) low-fat plain fromage frais, chilled**

Cranberry muffins

POINTS PER MUFFIN

3

points per recipe
35½

1 Line a 12 muffin tray with paper muffin cases. Preheat the oven to Gas Mark 6/200°C/fan oven 180°C.

2 Sift the flour, baking powder and cinnamon into a mixing bowl. Stir in the sugar and dried cranberries.

3 Beat the egg, milk and oil together in a separate bowl, then add to the dried ingredients, stirring well to mix.

4 Spoon the mixture into the muffin cases then bake for 15–20 minutes, until well risen and just firm. Transfer to a cooling rack.

Freezing recommended

- **300 g (10½ oz) plain flour**
- **2 teaspoons baking powder**
- **1 teaspoon ground cinnamon**
- **125 g (4½ oz) light muscovado sugar**
- **75 g (2¾ oz) dried cranberries**
- **1 egg, beaten**
- **225 ml (8 fl oz) skimmed milk**
- **50 ml (2 fl oz) sunflower oil or 'delicate' olive oil (for cakes and baking)**

makes: **18** slices   preparation: **30** mins + cooling   cooking: **2¼–2¾** hrs

points per recipe
55½

- **low-fat cooking spray**
- **125 g (4½ oz) dark muscovado sugar**
- **125 g (4½ oz) polyunsaturated margarine**
- **3 eggs, beaten**
- **125 g (4½ oz) plain flour**
- **a pinch of salt**
- **1 teaspoon ground mixed spice**
- **350 g (12 oz) mixed dried fruit**
- **75 g (2¾ oz) glacé cherries, halved (and rinsed if very sticky)**
- **25 g (1 oz) chopped mixed nuts**
- **finely grated zest and juice of ½ orange**
- **2 tablespoons sherry**

Christmas cake

1 Spray an 18 cm (7-inch) round cake tin with the low-fat cooking spray and line it with greaseproof paper. Preheat the oven to Gas Mark 2/150°C/fan oven 130°C.

2 Put the sugar and margarine in a mixing bowl and beat well until the mixture is light in texture and pale in colour. Gradually beat in the eggs. (If the mixture starts to curdle, don't worry – this will ease as you add the dry ingredients.)

3 In another bowl, sift the flour, salt and mixed spice together. Fold into the creamed mixture together with the dried fruit, cherries and nuts. Stir in the orange zest and juice, and the sherry.

4 Spoon the mixture into the prepared tin and level the surface. Bake for 2¼– 2¾ hours, covering the top with a circle of greaseproof paper if it starts to look too brown. Test to see if the cake is done by inserting a skewer into the middle – it should come out clean. If it does not, return the cake to the oven for a little longer, then test again.

5 Remove the cake from the oven and leave it to cool completely. Remove from the tin, wrap in several layers of greaseproof paper and store in an airtight container for 6–8 weeks.

Freezing not recommended

desserts,
cakes and bakes

points per recipe
7½

- **75 g (2¾ oz) ready-to-eat dried apricots, chopped finely**
- **225 g (8 oz) pears, peeled, cored and sliced into eight**
- **½ tablespoon clear honey**
- **25 g (1 oz) fresh wholemeal breadcrumbs**
- **15 g (½ oz) demerara sugar**
- **½ tablespoon plain flour**
- **15 g (½ oz) low-fat spread, melted**
- **a pinch of ground nutmeg**

Apricot and pear crunch

1 Preheat the oven to Gas Mark 4/180°C/fan oven 160°C.

2 Put the apricots, pear slices and honey in a saucepan with a tablespoon of water. Simmer gently, covered, for 5 minutes to warm through and soften.

3 Meanwhile, mix together the breadcrumbs, sugar, flour, spread and nutmeg to make the 'crunch' mix.

4 Spoon half of the pear mixture into an ovenproof dish and scatter half the 'crunch' over it. Top with the remaining pear mixture and then the last of the 'crunch'. Bake for 25–35 minutes, or until the topping is crunchy.

Freezing recommended

Apple batter cake

1 Line the base of a 20 cm (8-inch) round cake tin with baking parchment and lightly spray the sides with the low-fat cooking spray. Preheat the oven to Gas Mark 4/180°C/fan oven 160°C.

2 Put all the ingredients, except the brown sugar, apples and icing sugar, into a food processor or blender and whiz until smooth.

3 Sprinkle the soft brown sugar over the cake tin base then place the apples over it in an even layer. Pour the batter over then bake for about 1 hour, or until risen, golden brown and firm.

4 Remove the cake from the oven and cool in the tin for 15 minutes. Turn it out on to a serving plate and remove the parchment. Serve warm, dusted with icing sugar.

Freezing recommended

POINTS PER SERVING

3½

points per cake
20

- **low-fat cooking spray**
- **75 g (2¾ oz) self-raising flour**
- **1 teaspoon baking powder**
- **½ teaspoon ground cinnamon**
- **125 g (4½ oz) caster sugar**
- **100 ml (3½ fl oz) skimmed milk**
- **1 tablespoon sunflower oil**
- **2 eggs, beaten**
- **25 g (1 oz) light soft brown sugar**
- **500 g (1 lb 2 oz) Granny Smith apples, cored and sliced thinly**
- **1 teaspoon icing sugar, to dust**

points per recipe
19½

- **1 teaspoon instant coffee powder or granules**
- **1 tablespoon cocoa powder**
- **4 tablespoons hot water**
- **75 g (2¾ oz) good quality dark chocolate, minimum 70% cocoa solids**
- **2 eggs, separated**
- **1 tablespoon caster sugar**
- **2 tablespoons Tia Maria**
- **3 tablespoons whipping cream**
- **½ teaspoon cocoa powder, to dust**

Chocolate pots with Tia Maria

1 Put the coffee, cocoa powder, hot water and chocolate in a medium-size, heatproof bowl. Place the bowl over a pan of gently simmering water and stir until melted and blended. Remove the bowl from the heat and cool slightly by sitting it in cold water.

2 Meanwhile, whisk the egg whites in a grease-free bowl until they are just stiff. Add the caster sugar and whisk for a few more seconds until the mixture is glossy then set aside.

3 Add the egg yolks to the cooled chocolate mixture, then replace the bowl over the pan of simmering water and cook, stirring continuously, for 4–5 minutes, or until the mixture has thickened. Add the Tia Maria to the mixture, stir well, then fold in the egg whites.

4 Divide the mixture between six small pots or cups and chill in the fridge.

5 When ready to serve, whip the cream in a small bowl until it holds its shape, then spoon a little on the top of each dessert. Dust each pot with a little of the extra cocoa powder then serve.

Freezing recommended for up to 2 months

points per cake
24¹/₂

Hazelnut cake

- **3 egg whites**
- **175 g (6 oz) caster sugar**
- **1 teaspoon baking powder**
- **100 g (3¹/₂ oz) ground hazelnuts**
  For the filling and decoration
- **2 × 55 g pots of low-calorie chocolate mousse**
- **1 pear, peeled, cored and sliced thinly, or 200 g (7 oz) tinned pears in juice, drained**
- **1 teaspoon icing sugar, to dust**

1 Preheat the oven to Gas Mark 3/160°C/fan oven 140°C. Line two 18 cm (7-inch) non-stick cake tins with greaseproof paper.

2 Beat the egg whites until stiff then, using a metal spoon, gently mix in the sugar, baking powder and hazelnuts. Divide the mixture between the tins and bake for 30 minutes.

3 Carefully loosen the sides of the cakes with a knife and turn them out on to a wire rack to cool.

4 When cool, carefully remove the greaseproof paper. Don't worry if a little cake comes away with the paper.

5 Just before serving, turn one cake upside down on a plate. Spread the chocolate mousse over it thinly, and then layer the pear slices on top.

6 Place the second cake, top side uppermost, on top of the first and dust with the icing sugar.

Freezing not recommended

Chocolate sponge cake

V

1 Preheat the oven to Gas Mark 4/180°C/fan oven 160°C. Line the base of two round 18 cm (7-inch) sandwich tins with a circle of non-stick baking parchment.

2 In a small bowl, stir together the coffee, boiling water and granulated sweetener then set aside to cool.

3 In a clean bowl, and using electric beaters, whisk together the eggs and caster sugar until thick and foamy. Sift in the flour and cocoa powder and, using a metal spoon, fold in gently.

4 Divide the mixture between the tins and bake for 15–20 minutes, or until springy to the touch. Allow to cool on a wire rack.

5 Whip the cream until it forms soft peaks then fold in the cool sweetened coffee mixture. Use this to sandwich together the two sponges. Dust with a little icing sugar before serving.

Freezing recommended

POINTS PER SLICE
4
points per cake
31

- **1 tablespoon instant coffee granules**
- **1 tablespoon boiling water**
- **1 tablespoon granulated sweetener**
- **3 eggs**
- **100 g (3½ oz) caster sugar**
- **75 g (2¾ oz) self-raising flour**
- **25 g (1 oz) cocoa powder**
- **150 ml (5 fl oz) low-fat whipping cream (e.g Elmlea)**
- **1 teaspoon icing sugar, to dust**

makes: **8** slices   preparation: **25** mins + cooling   cooking: **45–55** mins

points per cake
36½

- **low-fat cooking spray**
- **50 g (1¾ oz)
  polyunsaturated margarine**
- **250 g (9 oz) caster sugar**
- **grated zest of 1 lemon**
- **250 g (9 oz) self-raising
  flour**
- **1 teaspoon baking powder**
- **1 egg**
- **100 ml (3½ fl oz) skimmed
  milk**
- **2 tablespoons low-fat plain
  yogurt**
- **juice of 2 lemons**

Lemon drizzle cake

1 Preheat the oven to Gas Mark 4/180°C/fan oven 160°C. Spray a 900 g (2 lb) loaf tin with the low-fat cooking spray and line the base with baking parchment.

2 Using electric beaters, whisk the margarine and 200 g (7 oz) of the sugar in a large bowl until the mixture resembles light, fluffy crumbs. Add the lemon zest, flour, baking powder, egg, milk and yogurt and mix until smooth. Spoon into the prepared tin and level the top.

3 Bake for 45–55 minutes, or until browned and springy to the touch. Cool in the tin for 10 minutes.

4 Place the lemon juice in a saucepan with the remaining sugar and 150 ml (¼ pint) of water. Bring to the boil, stirring until the sugar has dissolved, then leave to bubble for 10 minutes. Remove from the heat.

5 When the cake is cold, remove it from the tin and just before serving, pierce the cake in several places with a cocktail stick and then spoon the syrup over.

Freezing recommended at the end of step 3

Winter fruit bread

1 In a large bowl, mix together the fruit, almonds, flour, salt, sugar, lemon zest and yeast.

2 Make a well in the centre. Pour in the milk and melted butter.

3 Mix to a soft dough. Turn the dough out of the bowl. Knead for 10 minutes on a surface dusted with some of the extra flour.

4 Return the dough to the bowl, cover with cling film then leave to rise in a warm place for 2 hours until it has doubled in size.

5 Knead the dough again. Shape to fit into a 900 g (2 lb) loaf tin.

6 Cover the tin with cling film and a damp cloth and leave to rise in a warm place for a further 2 hours.

7 Preheat the oven to Gas Mark 4/180°C/fan oven 160°C. Remove the cling film. Brush the loaf top with the beaten egg.

8 Bake for 20 minutes, then cover with foil and bake for a further 30 minutes. To see if the bread is cooked, remove it from the oven and, using a tea towel or oven gloves, hold the loaf upside down and carefully remove the tin. Gently tap the base of the loaf. If it sounds hollow it is cooked; if not, slide the tin back on and return it to the oven for a few minutes then test again.

9 When it is cooked, turn out and cool on a wire rack.

Freezing recommended

POINTS PER SLICE

3

points per recipe
60

- **225 g (8 oz) mixed ready-to-eat fruit, chopped (e.g. figs, mango, apricots, prunes)**
- **125 g (4½ oz) blanched almonds, chopped**
- **450 g (1 lb) strong white bread flour, plus 50 g (1¾ oz) to dust work surfaces**
- **1 teaspoon salt**
- **75 g (2¾ oz) soft brown sugar**
- **grated zest of 1 lemon**
- **6 g packet of dried yeast**
- **250 ml (9 fl oz) skimmed milk, warmed**
- **50 g (1¾ oz) butter, melted**
- **1 egg, beaten**

Sticky toffee pudding

points per recipe
32

1 Preheat the oven to Gas Mark 5/190°C/fan oven 170°C. Spray an 18 cm (7-inch) square cake tin with the low-fat cooking spray and line the base with greaseproof paper.

2 Place the dates in a small pan with 200 ml (7 fl oz) water. Bring to the boil, then simmer for 5 minutes by which time the dates will have absorbed most of the water. Stir in the bicarbonate of soda.

3 Place the flour, sugar and low-fat spread in a bowl and rub together until the spread has been incorporated and the mixture is crumbly. Stir in the milk, vanilla essence and dates, then gently fold in the egg whites. Spoon the mixture into the cake tin and level the surface. Bake for 35 minutes, or until well risen and firm.

4 To make the sauce, place all the sauce ingredients in a small saucepan and heat gently until melted and smooth. Do not allow the mixture to boil.

5 Turn the pudding out onto a large plate and serve it warm or cold with the warm sauce drizzled over it.

Freezing recommended for the pudding only

- **low-fat cooking spray**
- **175 g (6 oz) stoned dates, chopped**
- **1 teaspoon bicarbonate of soda**
- **175 g (6 oz) self-raising flour**
- **175 g (6 oz) dark muscovado sugar**
- **50 g (1¾ oz) low-fat spread**
- **3 tablespoons skimmed milk**
- **1 teaspoon vanilla essence**
- **2 medium egg whites, whisked to soft peaks**
  For the sticky sauce
- **1½ tablespoons dark muscovado sugar**
- **1½ tablespoons golden syrup**
- **6 tablespoons very low-fat fromage frais**

points per recipe
29

Crunchy fruit fingers

- **50 g (1¾ oz) polyunsaturated margarine**
- **100 g (3½ oz) malt extract**
- **100 g (3½ oz) stoned dates, chopped finely**
- **100 g (3½ oz) ready-to-eat stoned prunes, chopped finely**
- **200 g (7 oz) rolled porridge oats**

1 Preheat the oven to Gas Mark 4/180°C/fan oven 160°C.

2 Melt the margarine in a small pan and stir in the malt extract. Add the dates, prunes and oats and stir until well combined.

3 Spread the mixture evenly in a shallow, non-stick baking tray then bake for 20 minutes, or until brown and beginning to firm up.

4 Remove the tray from the oven and mark the mixture into 20 fingers. Leave in the tin until cold.

5 When completely cold and firm, cut into fingers and store in an airtight container.

Freezing not recommended